For Shar...

Best Wishes

Cold Against the Heart

Poems by

Hugh MacDonald

National Library of Canada Cataloguing in Publication

MacDonald, Hugh, 1945-
    Cold against the heart / Hugh MacDonald.

Poems.
ISBN 0-88753-377-9

    I. Title.

PS8575.D6306C65 2003   C811'.54
C2003-902411-3
PR9199.3.M2513C65 2003

The Palm Poets Series is published by Black Moss Press at 2450 Byng Road, Windsor, Ontario N8W 3E8. Black Moss books are distributed in Canada and the U.S. by Firefly Books, 3680 Victoria Park Ave., Willowdale, Ont. Canada. All orders should be directed there.

Black Moss would like to acknowledge the generous support of the Canada Council and the Ontario Arts Council for its publishing program.

Le Conseil des Arts | The Canada Council
du Canada | for the Arts

ONTARIO ARTS COUNCIL
CONSEIL DES ARTS DE L'ONTARIO

Cold Against the Heart

Poems by

Hugh MacDonald

Black Moss
2003

Small Islands

When he was small
the island where he lived
stretched to infinity
far beyond the clover clad
meadows where he played.
Along the river's edge
close by his house
his dreams loomed large.
Off shore a tiny isle
red stack of sandy shale
wigged in squat spruce
graveyard for early pioneers
to which he liked to wade
at lowest tide
and stroll among the shades
brush past fragrant needled skirts
loving how the shoreline
boxed him in so he felt safe.
But as he grew, his islands
seemed to shrink
till he could see
how small he'd got
and still they boxed him in.

Down to the Sea Again...

At night I dream
the swaying deck
seasick even there
against the pier
in Halifax.
I come from an island
from a family
long upon the sea
and generations ashore
have left me unsure.
But once I set my feet
on hot plate steel
and feel the breast-like sway
of the living sea
I am born again
foetal sailor
son of the wind's kiss
the moon's embrace
and the relentless intercourse
of the inconstant tide.

Lonely Island

We learned—
at our grandfather's knee
from our parents bedtime
tale, and the slight-of-hand
of riddling priests who
bartered Hail Mary's
for ragamuffin souls
as they worked our
childhood streets
those love blind
merchants of dreams—
to long for the mystical
off shore island
wreathed in mist and fog
or that fertile Eden
floating overhead
beyond human knowing
awaiting those who
earn the right to
make safe landing there.

And we closed our minds
to other possibilities
knowing we were safe.
No one ever told us
what to expect
and so we dreamed:
    An islet of contemplation
    in drowsy silence
    or some mainland
    between whose shores
    we could explore
    boundless landscapes
    of the mind's devising?
    Or bound and spiced
    in a handsome crypt
    or an earth-walled hole
    or adrift in the air
    like the seeds of dandelion
    or soot from a chimney fire?

Likely though,
should we awake
we would find ourselves
ruefully alone
our passage spent
our vessels burned
longing still for
that other ending
lonely islands
whose yearning
loops the generations
locked in purblind
hearts and minds
thoughts and
dreams of thought
—nothing more.

9

Just Before the Fall

Something small and solid
lands hard upon the earth
a rustling is heard high
atop the tallest pine
on the riverbank
below his house.
Before that
the kind of shiver
that sneaks past
summer sunshine
to remind his bunched body
of seasons to come.
Perhaps the squirrel had
the same sensation
sudden urge to
climb closer to the sun
or perhaps resinous sap
piqued suddenly
inside his head and called:
"Come here and take me home."

10

Bunched and pungent cones
tumble branch to branch
land their hard green bodies
on needled earth beneath.
As winter seals the world
in ice, the cones will dry
release their tasty seed
and spring will come again
and then the fall and the next
death defying dance.

Changes

The Island sleeps
in its Maritime crib
like a fetal quarter moon,
its coast jagged and irregular
as a poor man's teeth
stained red as rust.
Where corporate farms thrive
once there were family farms
scattered like lupins
across the quilted landscape
where proud people
lived hand to mouth
cream cheque to
old-age pension
the roads muddy in spring
houses kerosene lit
until a bedtime just
before dark all year round.

Everyone had gardens
chickens in the yard
several generations
and a hired man
at the table for dinner.
Few had more than enough
but if you asked
how they were doing
they'd say fine thanks.
Life was too difficult
to be thought worthless.
Suicide was rare
and people were proud.
You'd never find
bored people
leaning on shovels
collecting stamps
to take them through
the long cold winter
the damp and ominous spring.

13

Because there was real work
that needed hard hands
and strong backs.
And in times of need
there were pies and loaves
pots and casseroles
carried through the door
and buildings and barns
raised in a day.
Most didn't have much
but what they had
usually carried the mark
of someone they knew
and it wasn't until
the summer season
when folks came back home
from The States with big cars
and fancy jewelry and clothes
that anyone ever felt poor.

14

Attraction

hoping to improve him
she gave her young admirer
a shirt
with "Magnetic Poetry"
embroidered
on its left breast.
Since then
she can't separate him
from her fridge.

15

Warm Thoughts

From early fall to late spring
the old farm house
was heated by a kitchen range
and two or three heaters
that chewed up wood
like farm boys eat supper.
When work allowed
Grampy and the boys
walked to the wood lot
with axes and buck saws
hard boiled eggs
sliced, buttered bread in wax paper
and a pickle jar of well water.
Work had such music then
the bucksaw sang its fiddle song
and the axe chopped out a steady beat.
Those were the silent days
before chain saws, when insects
and the birds had voices
and the leaves of trees and grass

were always heard to brush
and sway in perfect tune.
Boys and men could listen
as they worked or paused
and feel a part of all around
or talk when so inclined
without shouting to be heard
in this world of gentle noises
feeling strong and good
as their strong man-sweat
mingled with the smells of earth
and the blood scent of falling trees.

17

Manure

When you are twelve
and the day is warm
a pile of manure
can seem a mountain
an inanimate thing
lying like the leavings
of a glacier
on the hoof-worn ground
between the barns.
Your cousin Buddy
has parked the spreader
on the roadway
at your back
and you are the first
to take your fork
and break the sun-baked crust
which pulls away
like a well-formed scab
from the back
of some sleeping beast.

And you discover
you have entered
the steaming belly
of a living thing.
There are colours there
shades that run and blend
that ooze and bleed
flies and grubs
worms that curl and slither.
You could stand there
in wonder, and stare
but there is work to do.
And so you dig
and lift and toss
dig and lift and toss
watch the festering pile
shrink like mounded turnip
on a supper plate
feel the heat rise
as histories of life and death
arc across your shoulder
into the waiting spreader.

19

For all that is not profit
ends up here
that is not milk or cheese
or cream, or fat, or meat.
All that passes through
and does not pass the test:
the undigested bulk
the chaff, the seed, the stone
the drowned kitten
the fetal pig
the aborted, the stillborn
all here, all waiting
to be spread across the earth
to try it one more time.

20

Storm Day

Our wooden house squats
south face to the river.
Pine and spruce
fir and poplar
maple and oak
at our sides and backs.
Somewhere over Labrador
winter gathers ice in
northering teeth
blasts snow past our eaves
takes down the power lines.
Cold creeps in
through walls
ghostlike, penetrates
like neutrinos.
We wrap ourselves in blankets
toss a log into the fire
and hunker close
sneeze and wipe a smoky tear.
When dark comes
we light some lamps
make hot chocolate
on the wood stove
climb into our books.

Billy and the Rat

I don't know who set that trap
(One of those steel-jawed things
that could bite
off a small boy's hand
like a buzz saw).
Billy and I found it
upstairs in the granary
in a trough
in a sea of oats
when it jumped in the air
as we passed it by
kicking a scatter of grain
across our startled backs.
The rat clamped
in its rusted maw
was young and scared.
Be careful, it could bite
I said as Billy picked it up
and set it on the bench
along the wall.

"He's too hurt," he said
and opened up the trap.
Are you gonna kill it?
"No," he said, "His leg is broken.
He'll likely die
without my help.
You stay here
and watch him."
The rat lay
on the bench
and watched me
with squirrel eyes
his round tummy
rose and fell.
Billy brought sticks
and baler twine.
I watched him splint
the rat's leg
and hide him
where Grampy wouldn't look.
Every day we fed him
milk from a dropper

and bits of bread
talked to him
and touched him
like a pet.
The day the splint came off
Ratty was growing strong.
And maybe it hurt him
when we untied the string
made him lose his temper
and bite Billy
inside the thumb
where the skin is webbed
like a bat's wing.
Before Billy could think
his big hands moved fast
fingers strong
from milking cows
snapped that young rat's neck
and dropped him to the floor.
"Damn stupid rat," he said
and ran crying
out the door.

Spooked

Last night I go walking
just before ten
one of those cool
October nights
when the air feels
like spring water
and under the moon
I star in a dream
in black and white.
At the top of the lane
I turn toward town
walk the ribbon
of luminous pavement
between shadowed ditches
while a light breeze
sets grey autumn leaves
to silken whispering.
I come to the place
where the road
funnels between trees
hear sounds
like distant conversations

and I sense movement
in the shadows to my left
a shape like dog or fox
stares and does not move.
Several times before
walking past here
I recall a feeling
of being watched
a nervous memory
of having stopped
and searched darkness
for demon eyes
while shivers
teased my spine.
And here it sits
A glowing coyote
arms length away.
Coyotes fear a man
so I've been told
and I lunge at it
to make it run
but it sits and stays
I run again
this time straight at it

and it turns
and lopes away
just out of reach.
I start for home
the coyote close behind
and I think: rabies?
bite to the ankles?
I turn and lift gravel
from a neighbour's lane
and toss it
then another lane
and toss more.
The coyote stops
and sits perplexed.
I start again
almost running
until I'm home.
Only an animal
bored on an autumn night
lonely for companionship?
And why was I
a man who often walks
the roads at night
so much afraid?

Getting It Right

"The bucksaw will dance
if you get it right," he says.
"You take your turn
and then you rest.
You take me there
you follow me home.
You pull, then I pull
When it's my turn to work
you leave me alone
and I do the same for you.
Pushing a man
only jams the blade
and slows him down."
For a while
the blade jerks and jams
but Grampy won't quit
"Pull...release...follow
pull...release...follow.
Don't be a burden
on the bow of the saw.

Bear your own weight.
Let your arm ride
the saw's back lightly
on its return
like fingers on the waist
of a pretty girl.
Let the saw's teeth float
above the wood's wound
as an eagle rides the air.
Allow your mind
to write a song
upon the log between us.
Pull...release...follow
pull...release...follow."
And then I understand
the blade flies free
as a fiddler's bow
sawdust brushes past my legs
like dancer's skirts.
Grampy smiles.

Bivouac

I am nine and Billy thirteen. We plan
to sleep outside. We'll build a bivouac
in the wood across the road where we've
often walked in search of partridge
hares and grouse. There are clearings there
full of whispered secrets where leaves
tell lovely things they've seen to dancing
grasses, insects sing louder than crows
and distant jets. The night holds stars that
will comfort us like far off windows charm
the weary traveler. We will lie and watch
them wink 'till morning. I remember how
we built it, sappy fir trunk tied chest high
between two birch and shorter sticks
of wood to lend support to shedding boughs
of spruce laid layer on layer like cottage
thatch to ward off rain. We have a tarp
of rubberized canvas and woolen blankets.
Jackets rolled beneath our heads, Billy talks
awhile, explains things about girls he doesn't
understand then falls asleep. I lie awake
thinking, wondering why girls suddenly matter
and occupy such portions of our thoughts.

And then I listen to the traffic in the dark
around us where unseen creatures
move through a maze in moon shadow
paths, feeding on life and its potential
tender flesh, plants whose growth and
motion are toward light, which sway
in the caress of sun-warmed air, seed
or nut, fruit or flower. Billy's loud
breath, the heat of his back a comfort
amid night-fears fueled by the saw
of limb, the rustle of leaf and dry blade
hoot of owl, the woman scream
of the fleet fox, the scurry of panicked
feet through underbrush. The waxy moon
lights a village of eyes in the black hole
of a spruce top as somewhere far away
a trapper's dog finds the scent in the dewy air.
And then a long silence of woodland dreams
before the dive bombing motors of mosquito
wings fill my ears and I awake. The damp
of morning leadening the back and sleeves
of my clothes, the warm kiss of sun erases
the lights and frights of lurking eyes, brings
the sacrament of indelible memories
through the paisley walls of glittering trees.

Elsie's Things

A few years ago
I bought an old Ford Mustang
from the son
of a woman who died
a former teacher
and school principal.
It was a great car
hardly driven.
Last evening
coming home from town
in that same Mustang
upgraded
by two hundred thousand
kilometres of tire tugging adventure
I found the road blocked
at the bridge
near my home
by the house
that once belonged
to the same woman.
(It was being moved
to make way
for another fast-food joint.)

I sat for a while
in her car
looking at the white clapboard
on the side of her house
wondering if the situation
meant anything more
than a fine example of irony.
Rather than drive
the long way around
and returning later
for my son
at hockey practice
I returned to town
And had a coffee
At Tim Horton's
amused at how her car
was now deteriorating
along with me
and her house
(The house—which had experienced
a complete family life
including divorce)
was about to settle
perhaps for many years
on a new foundation
in a grove of pine.

Sliding Backwards

In my first marriage
my cars were all new
and came with monthly payments
the first a Pontiac Beaumont
parked in a paved driveway
outside a basement apartment
on Victory Avenue
in Charlottetown.
That car took Judy and me
on our under financed honeymoon
to New Brunswick and Maine
it waited outside the Panoramic View Motel
while we fought through
our wedding night
and she cried herself to sleep
and the Eden Rock Motel
the next night
after a chicken dinner
set me to puking all night.
And then it drove us

to school every morning
me hung over more than not
and moved with us to Montague.
I can't explain
what happened to us
I suspect much of it
came from my stupidity
and failure to notice
who and what she was
so our relationship
like that first car
ended up sliding
backwards into a post.

35

Cold Against the Heart

Yesterday I ended my walk
at the north-west corner
of our eight-acre field
next to the highway
where a tree line follows
an old farm ditch and dike
between this field
and a neighbour's
in a straight line
to the shore
of the Montague River.
I noticed a natural
opening among the trees
the size of a small room
and stepped inside when
young voices approached
along the road
three girls, two on bikes
one hustling beside
talking about the houses

where they lived.
I stood perfectly still
so as not to alarm
—guessed how they might
feel about a bearded man
lurking in a stand of spruce
just off the road.
When they were past
—voices echoing
only in my mind
as children's voices
tend to do—
I looked around at fallen
branches, moss and lichen
on earth's uneven floor
and there among the ruin
a single golf ball
white and dimpled
waiting to be found.
Last summer my son
had been here hitting
balls and dreaming

in warm summer air
and now he was away
working in Alberta.
He'd phoned the night
before, his ankle sprained
his heart strong.
He'd gained some weight
loved the work he did.
He thought he'd stay
at least another year.
I picked up the ball
and wiped it on my shirt
dropped it in the pocket
cold against the heart.

Panic Attack

That morning
he feels nothing
but fatigue.
At weigh-in
he is up a pound
and she is there
to give advice.
His second cup of coffee
yet his brain
won't stop sleeping.
The train he's on
won't stop ticking
down its tracks
though the scene
outside its windows
doesn't ever change.
On certain moments
he wants to be
anywhere else
but lacks the courage
to step off
fears the shadows
on the empty platforms
of the lonely towns
he passes through.

Something Lost in Matthew's Eyes

This time I see something
lost in Matthew's eyes
that runs away and shrinks
when it knows I'm looking
hides itself among
the rods and cones
or rides the optic nerves
to some grey fold
in the secret geography
where life's pirates
store the stolen treasures
of innocence.
And later in some reflected
vision of my own glance
I recognize a shadow
of the same something
risking a trip to the surface
of my own eyes
and I see how alike we are
remember the anarchy and fear

of my encounter with life
my inability to accept
the flawed perfection
of earthly things
the fear of falling
into cold and empty space
unwilling to paint my features
on the invisible canvas
of God's face
and unable to embrace
a faceless God.

41

Move Swimmingly

while the Ghiz family downstairs
(who owned that house
where Joe the Premier
had lately been conceived)
sat down to eat
my father paused
part way through a student paper
set down his red pencil
and turned to my mother
yawning in the doorway
(Earlier they had huddled quietly
at the top of the stairs
listened to the latest on the war
as the sound floated upward
from the landlord's Motorola
in the parlour down below.)
I'm going to bed now, dear
she may have said
handsome in tartan housecoat
cozy against October chill

something in the way she spoke
told him to leave his work
and toddle off to bed.
And though a son should leave
such stories here, I hope what my father felt
approached my bliss
on such nights with you, my love
your soft-skinned silhouette dark
against a freckled moon
howling out our ecstasy
as what became our children
moved swimmingly together.

43

The Difference Between Them

She wants them to fit
like Pangea—one large island.
He wants: his own continent
—a safe ocean between,
to send an exploring vessel
up a welcoming fjord
ford a shallow tickle
then sail away a while
feeling a part of something larger
than what he was before,
and he thrives on moments of loneliness
writes love poems with such conviction
while stranded in foreign lands

44

1973—74

I tried at first
to clear you from my mind
since I was not in yours
but you clung to me
like an odour that now belonged.
You would drift
from some periphery
and your arrival
stung the eyes
like atomized perfume.

45

Howl

Around three a.m.
the cat parks himself
under a bench
on the deck
face to face
with the neighbour's cat.
Their conversation
in a language learned
while being abducted
by verbose aliens,
eventually wakes me
and I turn from the window
in an attempt to escape.
It is early September,
a record-breaking
day of heat and humidity
and you lie beside me
on top of the covers
your skin white as marble,
one hand touching your forehead,

one round breast partially revealed
below your elbow.
My tired eyes
before closing,
snapping the image
which slowly forms and fades
and with the howling of cats
is lost in sleep.

47

New Years Eve 1972

Until midnight
you were invisible.
amid the two hundred who
milled around paper-draped
cigarette-scarred table tops
peopled with brown stubbies
tipped Styrofoam cups
broken noise-makers
stamped-metal ashtrays
abrim with yellowed filters
Export A, Cameo and Matinee.
Sequined purses sat
amid puddles while owners
in home-sewn sateen dresses
danced, then drifted off
in twos and threes
to piss and freshen up
in cinder-block washrooms.

We, the young husbands
smoked and swung
each other's wives
around the floor
in obedient, forced gaiety
one year's end like all the others
until the shout of zero
and our turn comes.
You and I kiss, while husbands
and wives, lovers
and sweethearts, friends
and strangers, sample the crowd
your tongue coming
warm and wet into mine
taking me like Lena's swan.
Dazed, I stopped
and watched you
move from man to man
unaware of how
our lives would change.

49

Mythology

Where love spilled
like Niagara Falls
dust billows
stings the eyes.

They bury their sins
in the soil of love
bright flowers
grow and bloom
(a crop
that laughs like children)
then break their own stems
and walk away.

What's left behind
is a dry and shrinking land
nothing will take root
or grow.

Morning Birth Song

He remembers
the softness of her glance
as she held their babe
against her breast
her eyes adrift
in the briny sea
of joy around them.
The sweat and stretch
of birth still undulant
in their senses. There is
a succulence about her
a moistness like glycerin
on the petals of a rose
the soft warm luxury
of milk pearled
in the raspberry sweetness
of her nipples
breasts, silken pillows
soft on apple cheeks.

The Body Discovers

The body discovers
it works best
when not alone
as I often was except
the radio hidden under
my bed turned low
searching amid the crackle
and snap for WKBW
and the top 40
at 1520 or on WPTR
or a Dodger's game
on CBS Radio
but that was before.
Then they sell the Dodgers
and I see your face
and everything changes
when we almost touch
and the static
draws me close like
paper pieces to a comb

and then my hands
feel the soft skin
of your arm or waist
as we dance and bop
float together
on the salty ocean
and when my mouth
touches your salty lips
a burning want is born
I have not found
words for even yet.
Simple things like
looking up at stars
get complicated then
so many things appear
that never were before.

53

Lumps

Before the lumps
and all that pain
he loved her breasts.
Waking and sleeping
they were in his eyes
and in his mind
hors d'oeuvres
soft scoops of vanilla
ice cream with raspberries
he loved to taste
playful puppies danced
and swayed before his face
finger food and candy
and all his favorite toys.
No matter how he tried
he couldn't see beyond
this fleshy fence
and he would start there
prefer them to her lips.
And sometimes she would say

You love them more than me.
After the pinch of mammograms
and the thrust of hollow steel
the pain, the tears and final parting
they said goodbye and he saw
them as they were: mere filets
emptied of the magic that was her.
And now when they make love
He feels the solid bone of her
his eyes glide past scars
to the wonder of her face
and so in love with her
and nothing comes between.

55

Interment

At the first chink of sunrise
he remembered
the long evening of rain
her fear compressing
the soft cushions of their embrace.
He wondered if she slept
or had lain awake
anticipating the slow chill
of elongated time.
It had been his plan
to stand watch on the night
writing a poem of perhaps
but he had been too tired.
And now the sun had closed
the lid and buried night
and all his dreams.

After the Rain

My pale island bleeds
like an aborted foetus
into the green Gulf

Descent to Charlottetown

After the downpour
my red rimmed island sheds
Its fading Joseph-coat
of landscape, bleeds through
silted arteries
into the saline Gulf.

58

First snow

Cooling armies
in white parachutes
subdue the earth

In the Air over Serbia

Terror is exciting; it can whet the appetite
The expectation of death heightens all the colours.

All the controls are here, remembered from childhood
The same games, but the blood wasn't real.

All blood. His up here pounding in his ears
Their's down below dozing on the train.

He can't see it yet. His eyes are on the bridge
For just a moment he remembers Nintendo.

The bridge must go. He locks it with his thumb
Fires and feels the missile go like premature ejacula-
tion.

And then he sees the train like Lawrence's snake
Crawl from some ominous hole into his life

Lurch and explode, tumble with the bridge
Into the indelible realm of lifelong insomnia.

His blood thickens, flows slow as mountain glaciers
While the blood of all the innocents below

Boils and burns to steam as toes and cheeks
Breasts and testicles dissolve into the paste of war.

Firebird

Sept 11, 2001

The firebird swoops low
brushes its shadow
across the backs
of workers in the streets
slips behind walls
of brick, concrete and glass
to reemerge as fire, and weld
its lost innocence
into millions of minds
turns to darkness
a hole in a Tower
the shape of a giant bird
a red cumulus of flame
and smoke, burning sparrows
lovers clutching hands and falling

Nothing Is Immutable

Nothing is immutable
in the physical universe.
The ethereal having more
sway over the future
of substance
than any tangible thing.
And even ideas exist
only as the content
of a mutable mind
passed on to mutable mind.
Or as a constantly eroding mark
on a mutable surface
with some form of mutable pen.
We have toyed with matter
for a few millennia.
We have carried knowledge
across several generations
but we too soon will be gone
and with us our self-proclaimed wonders.
And unless there is a God

there may be no mind
to mark our passing
or to record the coming
of a new age
of peace and prosperity across
an unmolested land.

Poetry in Motion

I form the reedited
page into a ball
toss it toward the waste
basket and miss.
It hits the floor
beside the white cat
who bats it up the hall.
It was my poem
until then, but now
it belongs to him.
It spins across the floor
and he skids after it
rolling happily
into the sunshine
below the tall window.
He sees the light
feels its warmth
across his shoulders
yawns and stretches
lies down to contemplate
the whole experience.
Such joy from mere ink
on a sheet of white paper.

Until Shrill Voices Called

I remember how we'd laugh
and fill the rooms with silly talk
and giggle till we couldn't stand
fine thoughts born and left to die
as if they didn't matter much.
Time was endless up ahead
and all the world as far
as we could reach was ours:
journeys had no need of roads
we roamed heedless of rules or signs
over lawns and picket fences
cold streams, ditch and hedge.
We seldom left for anywhere
without arriving somewhere else.
Obstacles were games to play
trees to climb, mountains of snow
to hollow out, to tunnel through
forts to defend from enemies
who were friends. And at the end
of every day, when shrill voices
called us home we'd always leave
excited and hungry for tomorrow.

Dark Thing

What is this thing
inside of me
I cannot understand
the dark and deadly part of me
that isn't heart or mind
that shapes the contours of my life
controls my very hand
and draws such luster
from my eyes
that I live mostly blind?

The Drawbacks of Creation

If you were a god
who was at first amused
with the creation
of a world
in perfect balance
but, being God
inclined to boredom
your powers without limit
moral or otherwise
and if you decided
to create a species
made up of two genders
that could never be predicted
or understood
even by one another
would you not
sit spellbound wondering
what will happen next?
And could you ever bring yourself
to turn the darn thing off?

Dandelions

The western world
has declared war
on the dandelion
that bright solar button
cheerful sign of coming heat.
There is a greening anger
I cannot understand
expressed in poisons
guaranteed to kill
new blooms of unsuitable plants.
But there are those
who long for them like asparagus
transforming them to salads
and syrupy rich wine.
I merely love their cheerful
intrusion on the canvas
of green around my door
I admire how they
send their children
off to see the world

in parachutes
how my children
gather them in love bouquets
how they bring colour
to all they colonize.
My lawn offers sanctuary
a launching pad to the lands
of irate neighbours
who think me merely
sloppy and lazy
who have no idea
of my malevolent intent.

In and Out of Harsh Light

Today I dared to walk
along my road
with both eyes closed.
I felt like the child
I never really
had time to be
as I made my way
by the sound and feel
of varied snows
below chirping feet.
I strayed into banks
built by passing plows
and then the other way
toward the yellow line
where snow and sand
were cut and pressed
by urgent wheels.
I tried to walk
the narrow path
on soft white powder

slowly pre-sifted
through champagne air
before settling there.
Mostly though
I felt like falling to sleep
drifting in and out of harsh light
away from the forms
I know too well
into the eerie silence
of blind whim.

University Naval Training Division

At H.M.C.S. Cornwallis
I learn to salute
men not worth
a sideways glance
and to move my feet
to a tuneless rhythm
not dictated by the soul.
This is not about the sea, I think,
but about weak men
training stronger ones
to be a wall that they
can hide behind.

God

I see god
as diversity
infinitely unknowable
outside of universal
manifestation
beyond the unfathomable depths
of deepest longing
glimpsed in the pools
of honest eyes.
Those who know God
as a personal servant
leashed at their doors
like a vigilant dog
have tied themselves
to something meaner than God.
Personal gods
might merely be the matter
found in our mirrors
the inversion
of something inside us
we wish were God
the momentary illusion
of reflected light
nothing
perceived as everything.

Graveyard

a glorious autumn day
in the graveyard
with its breezes and silences
its cadenced readings
and whispered comforts
the enduring green
of spruce and fir
and party dresses
for the dying
leaves of oak and maple
beech and birch
the carpet of lawn
between polished
slabs of stone
a poem I've lived before.
I grow more alive
as wounded earth
fresh-cut grass
and roses fill my nostrils

feel love and gratitude
for what remains.

Learning Not to Heel

Finding places
I didn't know were there
turns the colour up a notch
even in twilight.
A patch of grass
divided by a narrow path
where the rails once went
beside a road
I've traveled
hundreds of times
but never looked
beyond the verges.
I am just now
beginning to see past
those invisible fences
that have corralled me
blaming my imprisonment
on a choke chain
whose end I hold
in my own careful hands.

Fantasia in Five Short Movements
for B. N.

I
The second time I look upon her
I don't know who she is at first
don't understand why she draws my eyes
as intensely as the sun repels them.
With her, I think, also puzzled, looking back
as if she knows me from some other place.

II
It's safe to wonder from across the room
from where my eye finds pleasure
in anonymous contemplation of her face
the recognition of something half-remembered
of some lovely being invented for a book
who takes on flesh and steals my heart.

76

III

At her side I watch as a blind man
her blend of shades and motions
like those at work inside myself
her right hand circling above paper
perhaps casting spells with magic signs
below the willful roses of her cheeks.

IV

One amid a crowd in a darkened room
a glimpse of nature lit by lightening
wanting to stay but expected elsewhere
waiting for her promised music to begin
wishing it had been played only for me
I leave as cool rain begins to damp the yard.

V

Since then I feel her as a phantom limb
a hollow gnawing at the spirit's core
a notion born and lost within a day
that beguiles when I chance to think of her
a remembered song heard in a dream
short fiction based upon a single glance.

On Wolfe Island

Spring 2000

I'm at David Helwig's house
on Wolfe Island
in the spring
and I'm overwhelmed
by sunshine
after four days of rain.
I am overwhelmed
by birdsong
outside the windows
near the flowers
after the prison
of train and bus
and by the voices
of small children
in the garden out back
and by beautiful, long-legged
Sara in short shorts
who is building
something out of wood

78

while her children play
who is measuring lengths
of two-by-four
by stretching out
long and shapely legs
and standing like that
holding them in place
while she joints them
with a snarling saw.
And I am overwhelmed
by the coming and going
of the Wolfe Islander III
because I do not have
to catch a ferry
and with the skyline
of Kingston
fifteen minutes away by water
on the other side
and the constant heartbeat
of the composting toilet
and the buzz
of the black and white hornet

inside the window
of the lace-curtained white room
in which I'll sleep
in this old house
where everything
but me and the hornet
has been carefully laid out
to please the eye.

80

Just before Christmas, 2000.
Back from Charlottetown

For today
the steaming river
is far too fat
and fast to freeze.
The low west sun
invades the icy armour
of sleet clad trees.
The window view
is Neapolitan
layers of snow
and sky and rail
snow and sky
tree and ice
the sky orange
at its rim
fading to the blue
of aging eyes
full of young love.

What We Say about the Dead

He was dead for two weeks a while ago.
You can hear people talking, you know.
She wasn't sure if he smelled of liquor
or merely human fermentation.
Both, said her friend, the nurse, who'd heard
him too, but later insisted the man
had said "dead for two minutes."
But she claims he said two weeks
so the incident stuck in her memory.
The thought of being dead two weeks
and then coming back after listening
to what people had to say about
you after being dead that long could
change everything. There are things
she would like to know about death
but won't ask this man who once died
for two weeks and is back in "Emerg."
And she intends to be careful what
she says out loud the next time he dies.

At the Farmer's Market

the writers sell themselves
to one another.
They gather at a table
with coffee and smoked salmon
or a sausage in a bun
and talk of books
and others of their kind
publishers and dates of release
of tours, poems and stories
new stoves and wine.
They know the secrets
that permeate their lives
the constant and undying hope
that need for approval
from an ever-escalating
hierarchy of critics
the incessant rejection
the interminable waiting
and waiting

and waiting some more.

For Al

In our brief encounters
he appeared first
as an exploding voice
blind-siding me
like a pack of huskies
coming steam-breathed
through the darkness.
His words hungry as maggots
chewing to the bone of truth.

ma muse

Sometimes
it takes an outsider
to appreciate
the waves
that emanate from us.
Different people
too, can throw the switch
something in their voice
or the gravity
of their heavenly bodies
which touches me like
warm fingers on cool skin
spring water in a parched throat.
Muses I suppose
or just people
whose presence connects
to something in ourselves
courage or faith or strength
nature when she's sexy
or frightening
or just plain
breathtaking.

Ferry Reading
MV Confederation, Aug. 7, 2001

Children cry and
one Japanese family
jokes and laughs.
They don't know
why I stand manning
this microphone
in the crowded lounge
of the PEI ferry.
I read my words aloud
imagine they rise
like sun-drawn mist
form nourishing clouds
overhead.

Then fall
like
r
a
i
n

upon f   a   c   e   s
in the crowd.

To most
a brief and passing shower
soon forgotten.

But one woman
  watches
    her eyes
now moist and warm
hears me tell my mother's plight
comes home to live
with Mom and me
in the sad place where
that poem lives.

Poultry Reading

Marty opened his briefcase
in the dining room
at the Gillis Lodge
in rural Eldon, PEI
thumbed through
several thin books
marking pages with post-its.
I, his driver, sat and watched
along with two elderly ladies
who sat knitting at a table
in the rear. They whispered
wondering, I guess
who the strangers were
and why we had come
to this place where
all visitors are gold.
"What's going to happen?"
one of them asked.
I'm here for a poetry reading
Marty answered and smiled
continuing his work.

The women whispered
back and forth, their eyes
a blend of confusion and wonder.
"What did he say?"
the second woman asked her friend.
I'm giving a poetry reading
Marty said, trying to help.
And the women looked perplexed.
The first spoke again, cautiously.
"What's a poultry reading?"
Marty chuckled
A poetry reading, he said
stressing the consonants.
I'm going to read some poems
He held up the book
and everyone laughed
as we imagined him instead
opening and reading
the colourful entrails of chickens
and ducks, geese and turkeys.
as had the mothers
of these farm women
many decades ago.

Close Your Eyes Now and Sleep

Forget: the ever narrowing spaces
your growing children left for you
the dwindling vision of tired eyes.
Leave to them now, the next generation
the frightening awareness of diminishing returns.
You who danced until the final days
who wanted only time however thinly
to remain. How ironic your lust for a life
so simply lived, so repetitious, a tea
so weakly made, so briefly steeped.
There was so much you never saw
so many things you'd never done
each day lived out in familiar monotony.
All you ever wanted were signs of love
and there never was enough from certain ones.
And time has not done with those you left
their days doomed by winds of change
bearing seeds that together with you
they have sown but have not found their soil
but will, to bloom above them soon enough.

Last Dance

She lies face up
chin lifted high
eyes closed, mouth wide
like an ecstatic singer.
Moments ago the clouds
in the firmament of her eyes
allowed her a glimpse
of my face close to hers
her cheek felt my kiss.
And now I watch her
from my nearby chair
between pages I read
to soften the sounds
of laboured breaths.
And this time
her wasted arms move
graceful as a dancer's
the sweeping arcs
of the conductor
of an orchestra
only she can see.

Feeding Frances

The carrots are a mistake
cut too large and undercooked
I pick two small pieces and
lift the spoon to her mouth.
It amazes me how she knows
when to open, with her
eyes tightly closed, yet
with the slow approach
of the spoon her chin drops.
I imagine the games I
played with my children
the airplane approaches
the hanger, the car the garage
and the door opens just in time.
She smiles like she can read
my mind, hear my thoughts.
The spoon enters slowly and
her mouth closes, clears
it all, tries to chew and
swallow but can't, gags a bit

and opens her eyes wide to
look at me. Tears form and
fall from pale and cloudy corners.
I use the spoon to gently remove
what remains, softly saying how
I'm sorry, I should have known
and she makes noises that sound
like "It's all right." and smiles.
I try potatoes then, and pudding
and at the end remember how I fed
carrots to my children. I use my fork
to mash some carrot, mix it
with potatoes and she swallows all
with ease. I touch her forehead
kiss her and she falls asleep.

Mums

I should have known
potted mums
would not be right.
She always was
the practical one
grew plants we could eat
in our back garden.
But it was Mothers' Day
the blooms were bright
and I was blue.
I brought the plant
said, I love you, Mom.
She searched my face
for some clue
to this puzzling pot
smiled
as if she knew.
She grasped that mum
in wizened hand
pulled and tugged

shook and rubbed
down to bare roots.
I puzzled at first
thinking of myself
felt anger and hurt
until I saw
how sad she was
searching for meanings
she would never find.

TABLE OF CONTENTS